Northern M̲ and the **Harlem Renaissance**

Researching American History

edited by

JoAnne Weisman Deitch

Sheet music of song popularized by Bessie Smith. Raised in poverty in Tennessee, Bessie Smith became a national star during the 1920s.

Discovery Enterprises, Ltd.
Carlisle, Massachusetts

First Edition © Discovery Enterprises, Ltd., Carlisle, MA 2001

ISBN 1-57960-068-9

Library of Congress Catalog Card Number 00-110323

10 9 8 7 6 5 4 3 2 1

Printed in the United States of America

Subject Reference Guide:

Title: *Northern Migration and the Harlem Renaissance*
Series*: Researching American History*
edited by JoAnne Weisman Deitch

Nonfiction
Primary source documents re:
The Great Migration North - African American History
The Harlem Renaissance

Credits:

Cover Art: "Migration of the Negro" series,
panel no. 60, "and the migrants kept coming..." by Jacob Lawrence

Title page: Bessie Smith sheet music (National Archives)
Other illustrations are credited where they appear in the book.

Acknowledgments:

Special thanks to Kathryn Cryan-Hicks
for her research, editing, and introductions excerpted from
Pride and Promise: The Harlem Renaissance,
Copyright, Discovery Enterprises, Ltd., Lowell, MA 1993
and to
Mitch Yamasaki, Ph.D.
for his research, editing, and introductions excerpted from
Movin' On: The Great Migration North,
Copyright, Discovery Enterprises, Ltd., Carlisle, MA 1997
The introductory passages and primary source documents in this book rely
heavily upon and excerpt their work.

Contents

About the Series

Researching American History is a series of books which introduces various topics and periods in our nation's history through the study of primary source documents.

Reading the Historical Documents

On the following pages you'll find words written by people during or soon after the time of the events. This is firsthand information about what life was like back then. Illustrations are also created to record history. These historical documents are called **primary source materials**.

At first, some things written in earlier times may seem hard to understand. Language changes over the years, and the objects and activities described might be unfamiliar. Also, spellings were sometimes different. Below is a model which describes how we help with these challenges.

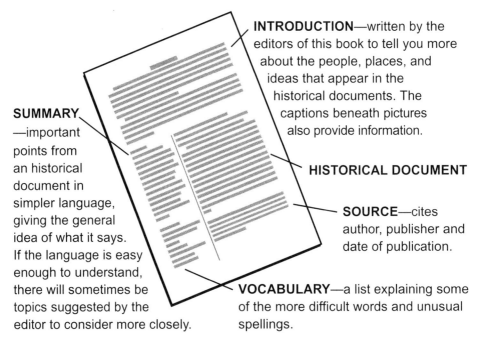

INTRODUCTION—written by the editors of this book to tell you more about the people, places, and ideas that appear in the historical documents. The captions beneath pictures also provide information.

SUMMARY—important points from an historical document in simpler language, giving the general idea of what it says. If the language is easy enough to understand, there will sometimes be topics suggested by the editor to consider more closely.

HISTORICAL DOCUMENT

SOURCE—cites author, publisher and date of publication.

VOCABULARY—a list explaining some of the more difficult words and unusual spellings.

In these historical documents, you may see three periods (...) called an ellipsis. It means that the editor has left out some words or sentences. You may see some words in brackets, such as [and]. These are words the editor has added to make the meaning clearer. When you use a document in a paper you're writing, you should include any ellipses and brackets it contains, just as you see them here. Be sure to give complete information about the author, title, and publisher of anything that was written by someone other than you.

Introduction

by Mitch Yamasaki, Ph.D.

Migrations have played a major role in shaping the history of the United States. The largest migration in the twentieth century took place between 1910 and 1970, when six and a half million African Americans migrated out of the South. Some of these migrants headed west. But most of them initially moved to northern cities such as Chicago, New York, and Philadelphia. In 1910, before the "Great Migration" began, over eighty percent of black Americans lived in the South, mostly in rural areas. In 1970, after the migration had ended, less than half of African Americans lived in the South, and only a quarter in the rural South. The two major causes for the migration were the "push" of hardships in the rural South and the "pull" of opportunities in the urban North.

Life in the South

At the start of World War I, two-thirds of African Americans living in the South were sharecroppers, who worked on lands they did not own, earning wages on a portion of the crops they produced. They purchased food and supplies from the landlord's commissary store on credit, the cost of which was subtracted from their wages at the end of the year. This often left the share-croppers with very little earnings or, in many instances, in debt to the land-lord. Southern sharecroppers were also plagued by natural disasters. In 1915, floods destroyed thousands of homes and farms in Mississippi and Alabama. Cotton, the principal crop grown in Louisiana, Mississippi, Alabama, and Georgia, was devastated by the boll weevil in the 1920s. Such disasters wiped out any hope for sharecroppers to turn a profit.

Although natural disasters and sharecropping caused hardships for poor blacks and whites alike, Southern blacks suffered under one other hardship— segregation. White-owned restaurants and theatres in the South either refused to serve blacks or segregated them in less desirable sections of their establishments. The U. S. Supreme Court decision in *Plessy v. Ferguson (1896)* permitted southern states to segregate public schools, parks, and transportation, provided that the facilities were equal. The South's "Jim Crow" laws created separate facilities for blacks and whites—but they were almost never equal.

African Americans who openly defied the South's racial laws and codes of behavior risked imprisonment and physical violence. Blacks who refused to step to one side when a white person approached, for example, were routinely jailed, whipped, or beaten. Lynching became the ultimate method of dealing with "upity" blacks. Over 1,100 blacks were lynched between 1900 and 1914. Lynchers were rarely prosecuted and those who were, were almost always acquitted. Despite the efforts of anti-lynching crusaders, such as Ida B. Wells-Barnett, lynchings continued into the post-World War II era.

"The Sharecropper's Settle"

The majority of sharecroppers in the South grew cotton. The cotton was picked in October and November and it was taken to the plantation's gin, where the seeds were removed and the fibers weighed. The planters packed the cotton into bales and sold it. After the planter did his accounting, the head of each sharecropper family was summoned to the plantation office for the "settle." The sharecropper was handed a piece of paper which showed how much money he had cleared from his crop. For many sharecroppers, the settle brought bitter disappointment. After paying for commissary purchases and other expenses, they often cleared only a few dollars, broke even, or owed money to the planter. For Moses Burse's family, the sharecropping system became a trap from which they could not escape.

> My dad...would get in debt and he'd figure every year he going to get out.... They'd tell you, "you bought so and so," they get through figuring it up you lacking $100 of coming clear. What the hell could you do? You living on his place, you couldn't walk off.
>
> Source: Spencer Crew, *Field to Factory: Afro-American Migration, 1915-1940.* Washington, D.C.: National Museum of American History, Smithsonian Institution, 1987, p.17.

Family, picking cotton in Jackson, Tennessee. (Library of Congress)

Planters usually blamed low cotton prices for the results of settles. Many sharecroppers suspected that planters were cheating them. Some planters were honest but others lowered the actual weight of sharecroppers' crops and/or "soaked" them for equipment repairs and commissary purchases.

Sharecroppers who felt cheated had little recourse. Southern laws always favored the landlord in disputes. Even to ask for a detailed accounting of the settle invited trouble—eviction, beating, or even lynching. Most unhappy sharecroppers simply left. Southern roads were filled with poor families after the settle, moving from one plantation to another. Unfortunately, the few plantations where sharecroppers regularly cleared good earnings rarely had openings. Most families therefore wound up in the same situation they thought they had left behind.

Views of the sharecropping system often depended on their vantage points. William Alexander Percy inherited a large Mississippi plantation in the 1930s. In his book, *Lanterns on the Levee* (1941), Percy states that sharecropping is the "most moral" of labor systems. He acknowledges that there are unscrupulous landlords that take advantage of sharecroppers, but he believes that steps can be taken to remedy the situation.

I happen to believe that profit-sharing is the most moral system under which human beings can work together and I am convinced that if it were accepted in principle by capital and labor, our industrial troubles would largely cease. So on Trail Lake [plantation] I continue to be partners with the sons of ex-slaves and to share fifty-fifty with [them] as my grandfather and Father had done....

Share-cropping is one of the best systems ever devised to give security and a chance for profit to the simple and the unskilled. It has but one drawback—it must be administered by human beings to whom it offers an unusual opportunity to rob without detection or punishment. The failure is not in the system itself, but in not living up to the contractual obligations of the system—the failure is in human nature.

(continued on next page)

Vocabulary:
contractual = connected with having a contract

Consider this:
What is the one drawback that Percy sees in the sharecropping system?

Consider this:
Explain what Percy meant by the last sentence of this excerpt. Give examples of your own to support what he meant by it.

Vocabulary:
boycott = to abstain from buying or using something, as a protest
Delta planters = refers to farmers located at the triangular area at the mouth of the Mississippi River
prey = any creature that's hunted, trapped, or caught

The Negro is no more on an equality with the white man in plantation matters than in any other dealings between the two.... If the white planter happens to be a crook, the share-cropper system on that plantation is bad for Negroes, as any other system would be. They are prey for the dishonest and temptation for the honest. If Delta planters were mostly cheats, the results of the share-cropper system would be as grievous as reported. But, strange as it may seem to the sainted East, we have quite a sprinkling of decent folk down our way....

Two courses of action would be effective against unworthy landlords: the Negroes could and should boycott such landlords, quietly and absolutely; the government could and should deny government benefits to the landlord who will not put the terms of his contract into writing, who will not carry out those terms and who will not permit the government to prove by its inspection that they have been carried out. In place of these suggested remedies, I can only recommend changing human nature. All we need anywhere in any age is character: from that everything follows.

Source: Escott, Paul D. and David R. Goldfield, eds., *Major Problems in the History of the American South*, Volume II: The New South, Lexington: D.C. Heath, 1990, pp. 111-4.

In her autobiography, *Coming of Age in Mississippi*, Anne Moody recalls her childhood, growing up in a sharecropper family.

I'm still haunted by dreams of the time we lived on Mr. Carter's plantation. Lots of Negroes lived on his place. Like Mama and Daddy they were all farmers. We all lived in rotten wood two-room shacks. But ours stood out from the others because it was up on the hill with Mr. Carter's big white house, overlooking the farms and the other shacks below.... Since we had only one big room and a kitchen, we all slept in the same room.... This big room had a plain, dull-colored wallpaper tacked loosely to the walls with large thumbtacks. Under each tack was a piece of cardboard which had been taken from shoe-boxes and cut into little squares to hold the paper and keep the tacks from tearing through. Because there were not enough tacks, the paper bulged in places....

We rarely saw Mama and Daddy because they were in the field every day except Sunday. They would get up early in the morning and leave the house just before daylight. It was six o'clock in the evening when they returned, just before dark....

The crop wasn't coming along as Daddy had expected. Every evening when he came from the field he was terribly depressed. He was running around the house grumbling all the time.

"[I]t was justa waste o' time. Didn't getta nuff rain for nuthin'. We ain't gonna even get two bales o' cotton this year. That corn ain't no god and them sweet potatoes jus' burning up in that hard-ass ground.... [A]h'd a did better on a job than this. Ain't gonna have nuthin' left when Mr. Carter take out his share." We had to hear this sermon almost every night and he was always snapping at Mama like it was all her fault.

Source: Anne Moody, *Coming of Age in Mississippi.* New York: Laurel, (1968), pp. 11-7.

Consider this:
Have you ever tried to write something using a dialect, or trying to capture someone's accent on paper? It's difficult to do. You have to listen very carefully to the way the person speaks, and then have someone try reading it back to you out loud. Try to get the flavor of the way this author's father spoke, by reading the last paragraph of this passage out loud.

Fifty Years

Although the Emancipation Proclamation delivered by Abraham Lincoln in 1863 was meant to make slavery illegal, equality was slow in coming. Poet James Weldon Johnson dealt with the issues in his poem, "Fifty Years."

Consider this:

The Emancipation Proclamation of 1863 may have made slavery illegal, but African Americans in the South remained enslaved in economic and social ways for many years after President Lincoln's important manifesto.

James Weldon Johnson looks back at the history of African American life. How does he show that blacks have earned the same opportunities and rights that whites have?

What is the poem's message of hope?

Vocabulary:

Attucks' = reference to Crispus Attucks, believed to be a runaway slave. He was the first man to die in the American Revolution at the Boston Massacre, on March 5, 1770.

ken = understanding, perception

ruthless = merciless

Fifty Years
(1863-1913)

by James Weldon Johnson

On the Fiftieth Anniversary of the Signing of the Emancipation Proclamation

O brothers mine, today we stand
Where half a century sweeps our ken,
Since God, through Lincoln's ready hand,
Struck off our bonds and made us men.

Just fifty years—a winter's day—
As runs the history of a race;
Yet, as we look back o'er the way,
How distant seems our starting place!

Look farther back! Three centuries!
To where a naked, shivering score,
Snatched from their haunts across the seas,
Stood, wild-eyed, on Virginia's shore.

. . . .

This land is ours by right of birth,
This land is ours by right of toil;
We helped to turn its virgin earth,
Our sweat is in its fruitful soil.

Where once the tangled forest stood—
Where flourished once rank weed and thorn—
Behold the path-traced, peaceful wood,
The cotton white, the yellow corn.

To gain these fruits that have been earned,
To hold these fields that have been won,
Our arms have strained, our backs have burned,
Bent bare beneath a ruthless sun.

That Banner which is now the type
Of victory on field and flood—
Remember, its first crimson stripe
Was dyed by Attucks' willing blood.

And never yet has come the cry—
When that fair flag has been assailed—
For men to do, for men to die,
That we have faltered or have failed.

And never yet O haughty Land,
Let us, at least, for this be praised—
Has one black, treason-guided hand
Ever against that flag been raised.

Then should we speak but servile words,
Or shall we hang our heads in shame?
Stand back of new-come foreign hordes,
And fear our heritage to claim?

No! stand erect and without fear,
And for our foes let this suffice—
We've bought a rightful sonship here,
And we have more than paid the price.

And yet, my brothers, well I know
The tethered feet, the pinioned wings,
The spirit bowed beneath the blow,
The heart grown faint from wounds and stings;
. . . .
Full well I know the hour when hope
Sinks dead, and round us everywhere
Hangs stifling darkness, and we grope
With hands uplifted in despair.

Courage! Look out, beyond, and see
The far horizon's beckoning span!
Faith in your God-known destiny!
We are a part of some great plan.
. . . .
Think you that John Brown's spirit stops?
That Lovejoy was but idly slain?
Or do you think those precious drops
From Lincoln's heart were shed in vain?

That for which millions prayed and sighed,
That for which tens of thousands fought,
For which so many freely died,
God cannot let it come to naught.

Source: James Weldon Johnson, ed., *The Book of American Negro Poetry*. New York: Harcourt Brace & World, Inc., 1922.

Vocabulary:

hordes = swarms of people

John Brown = Abolitionist, known for his attack on Harper's Ferry in 1859. He and his allies captured an armory in an attempt to free Negro slaves. He was captured, tried, and hanged.

Lovejoy = Elijah Parish Lovejoy, a minister and editor of an abolitionist paper. He spent his adult life (to age 35) defending freedom of speech, of the press, and freedom against slavery. He was killed by a mob in 1837, defending his press. For more about him, go to: http:/www.alton web.com/history/ lovejoy/index.html

pinioned = restrained by binding the arms

servile = submissive, like a slave or servant

suffice = to meet the needs or to be enough

The Migration North

by Kathryn Cryan-Hicks

White landowners managed to keep black sharecroppers in perpetual debt. Lack of education and training, together with the existing racial prejudice, made it difficult for black citizens to find employment with decent wages.

In addition to the economic inequities, African Americans at that time faced an increase in racial violence. Lynchings were on the rise and the feared Ku Klux Klan (formed in 1866) grew more powerful. Floods and the boll weevil brought devastation to many crops in the South, making food scarce.

It wasn't until 1914, with the outbreak of war in Europe, that many southern blacks were able to improve their situations. The War put a temporary halt to European immigration to the United States, and industry focused its recruiting efforts on the disenfranchised southern workers. Demand for labor in the northern cities provided a reasonable escape from the deplorable conditions in the South.

Opportunities in the North

For blacks suffering under the South's political, social, and economic oppression, northern cities must have looked like "the Promised Land." Wages there were, on the average, three times higher than wages in the South. There were no laws segregating the races. Nor were there poll taxes or literacy tests to prevent blacks from voting. Racial prejudice existed in the North, but not the constant fear, humiliation, and degradation that blacks lived with in the South.

Prior to the twentieth century, northern industries primarily employed native-born whites and European immigrants. World War I created a shortage of both these groups. The nativist National Origins Act of 1924 sharply curbed immigration from southern and eastern Europe. Badly in need of workers, northern industrialists set aside their racial prejudices and began to employ African Americans. Some northern companies sent recruiters to the South in order to attract workers. Recruiters painted glowing pictures of life in the North, often exaggerating the benefits of moving there. Recruiting was dangerous work. Southern planters, fearing the loss of their labor force, were able to get laws passed which banned recruiting in their states or municipalities. This enabled southern officials and vigilantes to hunt down recruiters.

Black newspapers, such as the *Chicago Defender*, exposed the injustices perpetrated on African Americans in the South. At the same time, they pointed out the advantages of living in the North. An editorial in the September 2, 1916 issue of the *Chicago Defender* stated, "The exodus of labor from the South has caused much alarm among the Southern whites, who have failed to treat them decent. The men, tired of being kicked and cursed, are leaving by the thousands." Many southern blacks saw the *Chicago Defender* as their guide for migrating to the North. The paper received thousands of letters inquiring about employment and housing. Following is a letter from Atlanta, Georgia dated April 30,1917.

The *Chicago Defender*

Dear Sir;

In reading the *Chicago Defender* I find that there are many jobs open for workmen, I wish that you would or can secure me a position in some of the northern cities; as a workman and not as a loafer. one who is willing to do any kind of hard inside or public work, have had broad experience in machenery and other work of the kind. A some what alround man can also cook, well trained devuloped man; have travel extensively through the western and southern States; A good strong morial religious man no [bad] habits. I will accept transportation advance and deducted from wages later. It does not matter where, that is; as to city, country, town or state since you secure the positions. I am quite sure you will be delighted in securing a position for a man of this description. I'll asure you will not regret of so doing. Hoping to hear from you soon.

Consider this:

Do you ever see letters like these in today's newspapers? The people writing to the editors here were desperate for jobs in Northern cities. What does someone do today when looking for work?

Things to do:
Find the misspelled words and the grammatical errors, and correct them.

This letter from Alabama, dated February 22, 1917, was published in the *New York Age*:

Will you please try to get me work in your city or anywhere in the North as a ladies' maid or even as a nurse for children or for an invalid. I have a little girl about ten years old. I would like to bring her along if convenient. I would like for the party to send a ticket for each of us, which can be deducted from my salary until paid. If you can find work for me, it will certainly be appreciated. While I have my preference and am qualified to do office work, I am willing to take what you can find for the time being.

Source: Trotter, Joe W. and Earl Lewis, eds., *African Americans in the Industrial Age: A Documentary History, 1915-1945*. Boston: Northeastern University Press, 1996, pp. 37-8, 35.

W.E.B. DuBois Reports on the Migration of Negroes

W.E.B. DuBois wrote of the migration of Negroes to the North in the N.A.A.C.P.'s paper, *The Crisis* (June 1917).

Consider this:

The data collected and reported by DuBois comes from many sources. How reliable do you think it is? What is the value in this? What types of sources does he cite?

Much has been written of the recent migration of colored people from the South to the North, but there have been very few attempts to give a definite, coherent picture of the whole movement. Aided by the funds of the National Association for the Advancement of Colored People, The Crisis has attempted to put into concrete form such knowledge as we have of this movement.

The data at hand are vague and have been collected from a hundred different sources. While the margin of error is large, the actual information which we have gathered is most valuable.

First, as to the number who have migrated to the North, there is wide difference of opinion. Our own conclusion is that about 250,000 colored workmen have come northward. This figure has been built up from reports like the following which we take from various personal sources and local newspaper accounts:

From Alabama, 60,000 able-bodied workers; from Savannah, Ga., 3,000; Montgomery, Ala., 2,000; West Point, Ala., 1,000; Americus, Ga., 3,000; Jefferson County, Ala., 10,000; West Point, Miss., 1,000; South Carolina, 27,000; West Point, Ga., 800; Macon, Ga. 3,000; Florida, 15,000; Notasulga, Ala., 3,000. From Abbeville, S.C., 'by the hundreds all through the fall and winter.' From Muskogee, Okla., '5,000 from the city and vicinity.' One day '1,022 Negroes from the South came into Cincinnati.' An estimate of the Boston, Mass., *Transcript* gives 200,000 immigrants. From Southwest Georgia, 5,000. Bradstreet's estimate: 'An immense migration.' From Birmingham, Ala.,

10,000; Arlington, Ga., 500; Waycross, Ga., 900; Bessemer, Ala., 3,000; Columbus, Ga., 500; Tuscaloosa, Ala., 2,500; Dawson, Ga., 1,500. Immigrants to Springfield, Mass., 500; to Chicago, Ill., 50,000, and 'coming in at the rate of 10,000 in two weeks,' (estimate of the *Chicago American*).

As to the reasons of the migration, undoubtedly, the immediate cause was economic, and the movement began because of floods in middle Alabama and Mississippi and because the latest devastation of the boll weevil came in these same districts.

A second economic cause was the cutting off of immigration from Europe to the North and the consequently wide-spread demand for common labor. The U.S. Department of Labor writes:

> *A representative of this department has made an investigation in regard thereto, but a report has not been printed for general distribution. It may be stated, however, that most of the help imported from the South has been employed by railroad companies, packing houses, foundries, factories, automobile plants, in the northern States as far west as Nebraska. At the present time the U.S. Employment Service is not cooperating in the direction of Negro help to the north.*

The third reason has been outbreaks of mob violence in northern and southwestern Georgia and in western South Carolina. These have been the three immediate causes, but back of them is, undoubtedly, the general dissatisfaction with the conditions in the South.

Consider this: What are the main reasons DuBois cites for the migration to the North? Which do you think was the most important cause? Explain you answer, using documents to support your position.

Why Blacks Left the South

Scholars and journalists at the time debated the reasons for the Great Migration. Most believed it was caused by the "push" of hardships in the South and the "pull" of opportunities in the North. The March 22, 1917 issue of the *New York Age* published a list of grievances articulated by southern blacks.

Vocabulary:

compels = forces

equitable = fair

franchise = privilege or right to vote, granted to a person, usually by a government

intimidation = threat, causing fear

legal redress = legal remedy

1. The "Jim Crow" car, product of the separate coach law that compels Negroes of every description to ride in one compartment of a railway coach, denies them the privilege of sleeping and dining cars, and in the case of street cars, obliges them to stand while seats are vacant on the possibility that some white passenger may get aboard.

2. The denial of the right of franchise, enforced usually by intimidation and mob methods.

3. The lack of equitable administration of school funds so that Negro children may be properly educated. At present Negroes pay their proportion indirectly in their rents, yet Negro schools receive in some cases less than 30 per cent of their just deserts, compelling Negroes to bear the added burden of supporting the many colleges so well known among them.

4. The segregation laws forbidding their residing outside of designated areas, thus leaving no natural expansion and forcing a fictitious value upon property rented or sold to them.

5. The generally neglected condition of streets, car service, street lighting, and other public utilities in Negro neighborhoods.

6. The denial of the privilege accorded others in the public parks and places of amusement. "For Whites Only" is a sign frequently seen in the South.

7. The abuse of Negroes by police officers, even attempts at explanation being usually regarded as resisting an officer, and as such rewarded with beating.

8. Lack of legal redress for insults offered to their women folks, and the generally prejudiced attitude of the courts.

9. The insulting and embarrassing treatment accorded the Negro patrons in many stores. A brutally frank statement often heard is "We don't serve niggers."

10. The remarkably low scale of wages offered to the Negro for his labor.

An African American social scientist working for the National Urban League argued that economic opportunity in the North was a stronger impetus for the Great Migration than the harsh treatment of blacks in the South.

After all, it means more that the Negroes who left the South were motivated more by the desire to improve their economic status than by fear of being man-handled by unfriendly whites. …Persecution plays its part—a considerable one. But when the whole of the migration of southern Negroes is considered, this part seems to be limited. It is indeed more likely that Negroes, like all others with a spark of ambition and self-interest, have been deserting soil which cannot yield returns in proportion to their population increase.…

Consider this:
What do you think the most important motivation was for blacks moving North?

Vocabulary:
persecution = oppression or harrassment

C. Otis disagreed with that assessment. Otis advanced his interpretation in a letter published in the October 1923 issue of *Opportunity*:

…Here is why he leaves the South: Unjust treatment, failure to secure a square deal in the courts, taxation without representation, denial of the right to vote thru the subterfuge of the white primary, no representation in any form of government, poor schools, unjust pay for and division of crops, insulting of women without any redress, and public torture.

Consider this:
Does Otis' theory make more sense? Why?

Vocabulary:
subterfuge = an evasive tactic used to avoid an awkward confrontation

Source: Adero, Malaika, ed., *Up South: Stories, Studies and Letters of this Century's African-American Migrations*. New York: The New Press, 1993, pp. 44, 48.

Bus station in Durham, North Carolina. (Library of Congress)

"Colored only" waiting room at a Florida train station. (Florida State Archives)

African Americans migrating north by train rode in segregated cars. Black cars were located near the locomotive. Windows could not be opened because of the soot and cinders coming from the engine. On overnight trips, blacks were barred from sleeping cars. They slept as best as they could on their seats, and ate home-cooked meals carried on board in baskets or cardboard boxes, brought from home.

Moving to Northern Cities

In *A Century of Negro Migration* (1918), Carter G. Woodson described the racial prejudice black migrants faced in northern cities.

Forced by restrictions of real estate men into congested districts, there has appeared the tendency toward further segregation. They are denied social contact, are sagaciously separated from the whites in public places of amusement and are clandestinely segregated in public schools in spite of the law to the contrary. As a consequence the Negro migrant often finds himself with less friends than he formerly had. The northern man who once denounced the South on account of its maltreatment of the blacks gradually grows silent when a Negro is brought next door. There comes with the movement, therefore, the difficult problems of housing.

...the migrants...are not wanted by the whites and are treated with contempt by the native blacks of the northern cities, who consider their brethren from the South too criminal and too vicious to be tolerated....

A large per cent of these Negroes are located in rooming houses or tenements for several families.... Many are crowded into the same room. ... Sometimes as many as four and five sleep in one bed, and that may be placed in the basement, dining-room or kitchen where there is neither adequate light nor air. In some cases men who work during the night sleep by day in beds used by others during the night. Some of their houses have no water inside and have toilets on the outside without sewerage connections. The cooking is often done by coal or wood stoves or kerosene lamps. Yet the rent runs high although the houses are generally out of repair and in some cases have been condemned by the municipality. The unsanitary conditions in which many of the blacks are compelled to live are in violation of municipal ordinances.

Summary:

The real estate men added to the problem of segregation of blacks from whites, by locating them in congested black neighborhoods. Where northerners once criticized southerners for their attitudes toward blacks, they really didn't want them to move into their neighborhoods.

The black migrants weren't trteated well by Northern blacks either.

So, many migrants were crowded together in shared apartments, with poor sanitary facilities.

Vocabulary:
clandestinely = secretly
denounced = condemned
maltreatment = bad
    treatment
municipal/municipality =
    having to do with city
    government/ city
sagaciously = wisely

Source: Adero, Malaika, ed., *Up South: Stories, Studies and Letters of this Century's African-American Migrations.* New York: The New Press, 1993, pp. 10-11.

In Chicago's north side, blacks often lived in two or three-story wooden houses, like the one pictured above; in New York, they lived in taller tenements. 1941 (National Archives)

Answering the Call to Arms

When the U.S. entered the first World War in 1917, 360,000 blacks, envigorated by their faith in democracy, put aside bitter memories of segregation and race violence and joined the fight for democracy. In New York City, the 15th Regiment of the New York National Guard made up of black soldiers (most of them from Harlem) was mustered into the regular Army, sent overseas to France and assigned to the French Army. Their regiment, renamed the 369th Infantry, was nicknamed the "Harlem Hellfighters." More than a hundred and fifty of these soldiers were decorated with the French Croix de Guerre, a military decoration for bravery.

After the War, black soldiers returned to the United States with pride and a new sense of themselves and of their place in the world. They had fought side-by-side with black soldiers from other parts of the world. They had won the respect of foreign nations for their bravery. They returned with the hope that the spirit of democracy that they had fought for in Europe would await them in the United States. *Chicago Defender* owner, Robert S. Abbott, had predicted too optimistically:

"The colored soldier who fights side by side with the white American in the titanic struggle now raging across the sea will hardly be begrudged a fair chance when the victorious armies return."

African American voices expressed the disappointment and the hope that they felt upon returning from the war. Following is a poem by Roscoe C. Jamison that appeared in *The Crisis* in September of 1917.

Negro Soldiers
by Roscoe C. Jamison

These truly are the Brave,
These men who cast aside
Old memories, to walk the blood-stained pave
Of Sacrifice, joining the solemn tide
That moves away, to suffer and to die
For Freedom—when their own is yet denied!
O Pride! O Prejudice! When they pass by,
Hail them, the Brave, for you now crucified!
These truly are the Free,
These souls that grandly rise
Above base dreams of vengeance for their wrongs,
Who march to war with visions in their eyes
Of Peace through Brotherhood, lifting glad songs
Aforetime, while they front the firing-line.
Stand and behold They take the field today,
Shedding their blood like Him now held divine,
That those who mock might find a better way!

Commentary:
Black soldiers had fought "to make the world safe for democracy," but their own country denied them theirs.

Vocabulary:
aforetime = previously
base = lowly
vengeance = retribution; punishing someone for something he or she did

The "Harlem Hellfighters" (National Archives)

Years of Strife
by Kathryn Cryan-Hicks

The years 1916 to 1920 saw over half a million African Americans migrating to northern cities. Some of these migrants were hired by war-related industries; some filled openings left vacant by workers who joined the armed services. Some were hired by companies whose regular workers were on strike. Many African Americans were employed for the first time and felt an economic security they had never known. In addition, they were able to offer family members in the South a refuge.

The refuge, however, was not always a safe one. The North had its share of racial violence.

On July 2, 1917, one of the nation's worst race riots occurred in East St. Louis, Illinois. Over 150 black citizens were killed, six thousand driven from their homes; and many homes were burned as the occupants struggled to leave them.

A few weeks after the riot in East St. Louis, over ten thousand blacks staged a silent march down Fifth Avenue to protest racial violence. With only the sound of muffled drums the children, all dressed in white, marched first, followed by the women all dressed in white. Then came the men dressed in black carrying banners of protest and a streamer which stretched the width of the street proclaiming "Your hands are full of blood." The parade moved in silence and was watched in silence by thousands of white citizens, many of them with tears in their eyes.

Vocabulary:

placards = posters

The Negro Silent Parade

The Crisis, September 1917

On the afternoon of Saturday July 28, a vast body of Negroes marched through the streets of New York in silent protest against the recent race riots and outrages. *The New York American* says:

"In silent protest against the recent killing of Negroes in race riots in Waco, Memphis and East St. Louis, 15,000 Negroes marched here yesterday afternoon. The parade formed in Fifth avenue and marched from Fifty-seventh street to Madison Square.

"Placards carried by boy scouts, aged men and by women and children explained the purpose of the demonstration.

"A detailed account of the causes for which the parade was held is given as follows by the *New York Times:*

"During the progress of the march circulars were distributed among the crowds telling of the purpose which brought the Negroes together. Under the caption, 'Why Do We March?' the circular read, in part, as follows:

'We march because by the grace of God and the force of truth the dangerous, hampering walls of prejudice and inhuman injustices must fall.

'We march because we want to make impossible a repetition of Waco, Memphis, and East St. Louis by arousing the conscience of the country, and to bring the murderers of our brothers, sisters and innocent children to justice.

'We march because we deem it a crime to be silent in the face of such barbaric acts.

'We march because we are thoroughly opposed to Jim Crow cars, etc., segregation, discrimination, disfranchisement, lynching, and the host of evils that are forced on us. It is time that the spirit of Christ should be manifested in the making and execution of laws.

'We march because we want our children to live in a better land and enjoy fairer conditions than have fallen to our lot.

'We march in memory of our butchered dead, the massacre of honest toilers who were removing the reproach of laziness and thriftlessness hurled at the entire race. They died to prove our worthiness to live. We live in spite of death shadowing us and ours. We prosper in the face of the most unwarranted and illegal oppression.

'We march because the growing consciousness and solidarity of race, coupled with sorrow and discrimination, have made us one; a union that may never be dissolved in spite of shallow-

(continued on next page)

Vocabulary:
barbaric = crude or wild
hampering = hindering
oppression = persecution
reproach = blame
solidarity = union of
    interests, beliefs
thriftlessness = wise
    management of money
unwarranted = groundless,
    having no justification

On July 28, 1917, in New York City, following a massacre of blacks in East St. Louis, Illinois, thousands marched in silent protest of the violent and discriminatory treatment of blacks in America. (National Archives)

Vocabulary:

agitators = people who disturb something

pundits = learned people

brained agitators, scheming pundits and political tricksters who secure a fleeting popularity and uncertain financial support by promoting the disunion of a people who ought to consider themselves as one.'

"Although the paraders marched by in silence their sentiments were proclaimed by many mottoes, a complete list of which follows:

'Memphis and Waco-Centers of American Culture?'

'Alabama needs 75,000 Ballots to elect 10 Congressmen. Minnesota needs 300,000. How do they do it?'

'350,000 voters in the South have as much political power as the 1,500,000 voters of New York State. How do they do it?'

'Each white man in the South by disfranchising the black working man casts from 3 to 13 times as many ballots as YOU.'

'Georgia and New Jersey have the same vote for President. Georgia casts 80,000 votes; New Jersey casts 430,00O.'

'Make America safe for Democracy.'

'Taxation without representation is tyranny.'

'Thou shalt not kill.'

'Thou shalt not bear false witness against thy neighbor.'

'We hold these truths to be self-evident that all men are created equal. That they are endowed by their Creator with certain unalienable rights. That among these are LIFE, LIBERTY and the pursuit of HAPPINESS.'

'If you are of African descent tear off this corner.'

'America has lynched without trial 2,867 Negroes in 31 years and not a single murderer has suffered.'

'200,000 black men fought for your liberty in the Civil War'

'The first blood for American Independence was shed by a Negro-Crispus Attucks.'

'We have fought for the liberty of white Americans in 6 wars; our reward is East St. Louis.'

'12,000 of us fought with Jackson at New Orleans.'

Things to do:
Choose one of the sayings from the placards that were carried in the silent parade and explain the refernces and /or the significance of its meaning. How does it relate to civil rights issues?

Vocabulary:
unalienable = not to be
    separated

The Chicago Riot of 1919

St. Clair Drake and Horace Cayton examined the forces that led to the Chicago riot in their book *Black Metropolis: A Study of Negro Life in a Northern City* (1945).

Consider this:

Have you ever been discriminated against because of age, race, gender, nationality, or religion? Write an essay or a short story based on your experience(s). How did it feel to be treated in this way? Do you think attitudes toward discrimination are changing in the 21st century? Explain.

Vocabulary:

altercation = a heated quarrel

ensuing = immediately following

The Chicago riot began on a hot July day in 1919 as the result of an altercation at a bathing beach. A colored boy swam across the imaginary line which was supposed to separate Negroes from whites at the Twenty-ninth Street beach. He was stoned by a group of white boys. During the ensuing argument between groups of Negro and white bathers, the boy was drowned. Colored bathers were enraged....

"White people have killed a Negro." The resulting fight...set off six days of rioting...took at least thirty-eight lives, resulted in over five hundred injuries, destroyed $250,000 worth of property, and left over a thousand persons homeless.

Source: Joanne Grant, ed., *Black Protest: History, Documents and Analyses*. New York: Fawcett Premier, 1991, pp.187-8.

Jobs in the North

Factory Jobs

Otto Hall, Director of the Negro Department of the Trade Union Educational League (T.U.E.L.), pointed out the difficulties black workers faced in northern industries.

Since the great majority of Negro workers are unskilled and unorganized, they suffer more intensely than any other group from the effects of rationalism.

They suffer from double oppression, being oppressed as Negroes and as workers.

They are the last to be hired and are always the first to be fired. In every shop, mill, or factory they are given the worst jobs.

Negro workers are always the lowest paid workers in all industries. The worst and lowest paid jobs are considered "Negro jobs" and the better jobs are for the whites.

The Negro worker, no matter how capable, is seldom allowed to step into what is considered by the employers as a white man's job.

In the industrial centers to which these workers migrate, they are forced into the worst houses in the worst districts and pay the highest rents in spite of the low wages that they receive.

Because of the small earnings of the men the wives and children are forced to work in sweat shops and in the fields under the most miserable conditions.

Source: Otto Hall, *Daily Worker,* April 6, 1920. Found in Foner, Eric and Ronald Lewis, eds., *Black Workers: A Documentary History from Colonial Times to the Present,* Philadelphia: Temple University Press, 1989. p. 426.

Vocabulary:

rationalism = the theory that reason, rather than authority, is the only real basis for beliefs

sweat shop = a shop or factory where employees work under bad conditions for long hours and low pay

Black Workers and Unions

Otto Hall believed that black workers had to organize "together with the fighting unions of white workers who are willing to fight together with us to better the conditions of the working class as a whole." Hall's 1920 article in the *Daily Worker* warns against turning to the AFL (American Federation of Labor, founded in 1886) for support. It was built on the principle of organizing skilled workers into craft unions, and was not receptive to unskilled workers, whom it saw as easily replaced during strikes. It also generally excluded blacks and women. An excerpt from his article follows.

Vocabulary:

affiliated = associated with

We all know about the American Federation of Labor and its policy towards the Negro worker. In spite of its general constitution and declaration, that it does not discriminate against the Negro, its affiliated bodies do, and during its 40 years or more of existence it has never made a serious effort to organize the Negro workers....

...The Trade Union Educational League and those who support it are the only organizations that have carried on a fight for the organization of all workers regardless of race, nationality or color. Its policy in the various unions has been to carry on a consistent fight for the admittance of Negroes and the breaking up of the exclusion policy of these fakers for many years.

Source: Otto Hall, *Daily Worker,* 1920. Found in Foner, Eric and Ronald Lewis, eds., *Black Workers: A Documentary History from Colonial Times to the Present*, Philadelphia: Temple University Press, 1989. p. 427.

In the November 1929 issue of *Opportunity*, Elmer Anderson Carter answers assertions that black workers are "unorganizable."

Vocabulary:

asserted = stated

doctrines = principles that are taught

exploited = taken advantage of

feeble = weak; lacking vigor or force

It is often asserted that black workers have been slow in accepting the doctrines and methods of organized labor. The most exploited workers in the United States, they have remained the least organized and therefore the most feeble in achieving either security and their employment or living wages and decent working conditions. This apparent indifference of the black worker to the benefits of trade unionism has served to draw the fire of various officials of the American Federation of Labor who, when accused of apathy to the fate of Negro labor, have replied from time to time that the Negro worker was unorganizable, and was as yet incapable of appreciating the necessity of identifying himself with the American Labor Movement.

...The Negro, contrary to general opinion, is not slow to oganize. There are approximately 100,000 Negro workers who are affiliated with some form of labor organization, a remarkable number when one considers that the Negro not only is outside of the pale of the skilled craft organizations, but also is compelled oft time to face the opposition of white labor, organized and unorganized, in order to gain a foothold in industry.

Vocabulary:
apathy = indifference; lack of emotion or feeling
outside of the pale = unacceptable to (usually phrased "beyond the pale")

Source: Foner, Eric and Ronald Lewis, eds., *Black Workers: A Documentary History from Colonial Times to the Present.* Philadelphia: Temple Univ. Press, 1989, pp. 408-9.

Founded in 1935, the Congress of Industrial Organizations (CIO) attempted to organize workers rejected by the AFL. The CIO's constitution attests to its inclusive philosophy. Unlike the AFL, the CIO actively courted black workers.

The objects of the organization are:
To bring about the effective organization of the working men and women of America regardless of race, creed, color or nationality, and to unite them for common action into labor unions for their mutual aid and protection.

The September 18, 1937 issue of the *Pittsburgh Courier* notes the success of the CIO prompted the AFL to reconsider its attitude towards black workers.

In the face of the success of the CIO, the A.F. of L. unions have in many instances abandoned their traditional attitude of indifference to Negro labor which frequently bordered on hostility, and are often as eager to eliminate every trace of color discrimination as the CIO organizations.

When the AFL and CIO merged in 1955, its constitution declared that one of its principles was "To encourage all workers without regard to race, creed, color or national origin to share in the full benefits of union organization."

Women in the Work Force

In the rural South, African American women worked in the fields alongside their fathers, husbands, and sons. Before going to the fields, women fixed breakfast, and washed and hung their families' clothes. When they came home from the fields, women prepared dinner, cleaned their houses, and sewed and ironed their families' clothes.

In order to supplement their families' income, some black women took in other people's washing and ironing. Others worked for white families as cooks, maids, and nannies. Domestic work was dominated by black women because white women generally shunned such jobs. As a result of financial need, black women in the North as well as the South were four times more likely to be in the work force than white women. In a 1981 interview, Priscilla Butler recalls working for a white lawyer's family in Mobile, Alabama in the 1930s.

Consider this:

In what situation, if any, would you be willing to work extra hours without additional pay?

I went to work for this lawyer and they paid you ten a week, and oh, that was a lot of money then. But darling! You stayed there. If they wanted to have a conversation around the table, you didn't act sour, didn't rattle those pots and pans. And maybe it be nine-thirty before you'd get out of the kitchen. And oh, my dear, you'd been there since six-thirty in the morning.

Source: Susan Tucker, *Telling Memoirs Among Southern Women: Domestic Workers and their Employers in the Segregated South.* New York: Schocken Books, 1988, p. 24.

The majority of black women working in the North were "domestics." (National Archives)

More job opportunities opened up for African American women who migrated to the North. In a 1938 bulletin for the U.S. Department of Labor entitled "The Negro Woman Worker," Jean Collier Brown points out the problems they faced in the work place.

Though women in general have been discriminated against and exploited through limitation of their opportunities for employment, through long hours, low wages, and harmful working conditions, such hardships have fallen upon Negro women with double harshness. As the members of a new and inexperienced group arrive at the doors of industry, the jobs that open up to them ordinarily are those vacated by other workers who move on to more highly paid occupations. Negro women have formed such a new and inexperienced group of wage employment. To their lot, therefore, have fallen the more menial jobs, the lower-paid, the more hazardous—in general, the least agreeable and desirable. And one of the tragedies of the depression was the realization that the unsteady foothold Negro women had attained in even these jobs was lost when great numbers of unemployed workers from other fields clamored for employment.

Vocabulary:

menial jobs = jobs appropriate for servants

Source: Foner, Eric and Ronald Lewis, eds., *Black Workers: A Documentary History from Colonial Times to the Present.* Philadelphia: Temple University Press, 1989, p. 365.

Mary Louise Williams recounts the struggles she went through in order to earn a living in the July 1923 issue of *The Messenger:*

My working career started a few years back in a small city in New York State, with a high school education. After graduation, being filled with the enthusiasm of youth, I naturally turned my thoughts to "something different."

I applied to several offices of employment, seeking even as inferior a position as addressing envelopes. At every place I met with disappoint-

(continued on next page)

Consider this:

What does she mean by the phrase — "By this I felt somewhat like a peacock who had looked at his feet"?

ment. None felt they could use colored help in that capacity.

By this I felt somewhat like a peacock who had looked at his feet. Now, I worked around at odd jobs and housework until one day I received a surprise. Through the kind intercession of the Vice-President of a manufactory I was given an opportunity in its perfume department. I was to act as forelady and stock clerk. The management, being so well pleased, doubled my salary after a year's service....

[One day, a fellow worker met Mary's mother, who, unlike Mary was obviously colored.]

Consider this:

Why did Mr. T. want a Negro employee who looked very black? Is this practice allowed today?

Vocabulary:

bootblack = a person who cleans and polishes shoes for a living

chagrin = embarrassment; humiliation

Next morning I was summoned to the office. You can imagine my surprise upon finding my services were no longer needed. Mr. Vice-President softened it as best he could: "There is no fault with your work, but the girls will not work with a Negro. We would gladly keep you if we could, but it is better to lose one girl than to lose twenty."

On another occasion I answered an advertisement in the paper worded thus:"Wanted: a colored girl, high school graduate preferred. Apply Dey's Department Store." I dressed with care expecting to find at least a sales lady's opening. Just picture for yourself my chagrin upon learning they desired a bootblack in the ladies' rest room! The reason they wanted an educated girl was to keep their wealthy customers from coming into contact with objectionable Negroes. I had no chance to refuse the job because Mr. T. said I looked too much like a Caucasian and he could not use me. He finally hired a high school graduate who had trained two years for a teacher. Is it not a pity that a colored girl must be educated to qualify as a bootblack?"

Source: Foner, Eric and Ronald Lewis, eds., *Black Workers: A Documentary History from Colonial Times to the Present.* Philadelphia: Temple University Press, 1989, pp. 389-90.

Strategies on Race Relations

Booker T. Washington

When the Civil War ended in 1865, Booker T. Washington was a nine-year-old slave on a farm near Hale's Ford, Virginia. He struggled to get a good education, which included graduation from the Hampton Institute, a school for southern blacks run by northern philanthropists. In 1881, Washington founded Tuskegee Institute in Alabama to provide vocational training for African Americans. His school received extensive backing from wealthy and powerful whites. Washington emphasized immediate self-improvement within the South's segregated system, rather than agitating for equality and desegregation. He expressed this philosophy in an address at the 1895 Atlanta Exposition, a speech which came to be known as the "Atlanta Compromise."

To those of my race who depend on bettering their condition in a foreign land or who underestimate the importance of cultivating friendly relations with the Southern white man, who is their next-door neighbor, I would say: Cast down your bucket where you are; cast it down in making friends, in every manly way, of the people of all races by whom we are surrounded. Cast it down in agriculture, mechanics, in commerce, in domestic service, and in the professions....

Our greatest danger is that, in the great leap from slavery to freedom, we may overlook the fact that the masses of us are to live by the productions of our hands and fail to keep in mind that we shall prosper in proportion as we

Summary:

For those blacks who want to improve their relationships in other lands or with Southern whites, I recommend you stay where you are and work at what you know how to do.

Our greatest danger, now that we have our freedom, is to overlook the fact that most of us have to make a living with our hands [not with our minds.]

(continued on next page)

Summary:
We have to work at useful occupations. There is as much dignity in farming as there is in writing poetry. We must begin at the bottom, not the top.

To the whites, we say that we have shown loyalty and support for you and your families in the past, and so we will in the future. We can work with you, but still remain separate in a social sense.

learn to dignify and glorify common labor, and put brains and skill into the common occupations of life; shall prosper in proportion as we learn to draw the line between the superficial and the substantial, the ornamental gewgaws of life and the useful. No race can prosper till it learns that there is as much dignity in tilling a field as in writing a poem. It is at the bottom of life we must begin, and not at the top. Nor should we permit our grievances to overshadow our opportunities.

To those of the white race...as we have proved our loyalty to you in the past, in nursing your children, watching by the sickbed of your mothers and fathers, and often following them with tear-dimmed eyes to their graves, so in the future, in our humble way, we shall stand by you with a devotion that no foreigner can approach, ready to lay down our lives, if need be, in defense of yours; interlacing our industrial, commercial, civil and religious life with yours in a way that shall make the interests of both races one. In all things that are purely social we can be as separate as the fingers, yet one as the hand in all things essential to mutual progress.

In his autobiography, *Up From Slavery* (1901), Washington preached patience to blacks anxious to gain political equality.

Summary:
Negroes should conduct themselves modestly as regards making political claims. For the Negro to have political rights will take a long time.

Vocabulary:
deport = to behave or conduct oneself

I believe it is the duty of the Negro—as the greater part of the race is already doing—to deport himself modestly in regard to political claims, depending upon the slow but sure influences that proceed from the possession of property, intelligence, and high character for the full recognition of his political rights. I think that the according of the full exercise of political rights is going to be a matter of natural, slow growth, not an over-night, gourd-vine affair.

Source: William Dudley, ed., *African Americans: Opposing Viewpoints.* San Diego: Greenhaven Press, 1997, pp. 136-40.

W.E.B. DuBois

(UPI photo)

Born in Massachusetts three years after the end of the Civil War, W.E.B. DuBois was the first African American to earn a Ph.D. from Harvard University. In time, DuBois became a prominent critic of Washington's "Atlanta Compromise." He believed that the only way blacks could attain equality was through agitation. In 1905, DuBois and about thirty like-minded blacks met at Niagara Falls to plan their strategy for advancing their cause. His group merged with a bi-racial group advocating African American rights to form the National Association for the Advancement of Colored People (NAACP) in 1909. Most of the top posts went to whites, but DuBois became the editor of the organization's journal—*The Crisis.* DuBois' thoughts on race relations, including his criticism of Washington, are found in his book *The Souls of Black Folk* (1903).

Mr. Washington represents in Negro thought the old attitude of adjustment and submission.... In the history of nearly all other races and peoples the doctrine preached at such crises has been that manly self-respect is worth more than lands and houses, and that a people who voluntarily surrender such respect, or cease striving for it, are not worth civilizing.

In answer to this, it has been claimed that the Negro can survive only through submission. Mr. Washington distinctly asks that black people give up, at least for the present, three things, — First, political power,
Second, insistence on civil rights,

(continued on next page)

Consider this:

How does DuBois' attitude toward Negro advancement differ from Booker T. Washington's? Which do you agree with and why?

Vocabulary:

submission = yielding power or authority to another

Vocabulary:

advocated =
    recommended
caste = a social class
    separated by heredity
    or profession
fain = preferably, gladly
servile = slavish,
    submissive
tender = offer

Third, higher education of Negro youth, —
and concentrate all their energies on industrial
education, the accumulation of wealth, and the
conciliation of the South. This policy has been
courageously and insistently advocated for over
fifteen years, and has been triumphant for per-
haps ten years. As a result of this tender of the
palm-branch, what has been the return? In these
years there have occurred:

1. The disenfranchisement of the Negro.
2. The legal creation of a distinct status of civil
    inferiority for the Negro.
3. The steady withdrawal of aid from institu-
    tions for the higher training of the Negro.

These movements are not, to be sure, direct
results of Mr. Washington's teachings; but his
propaganda has, without a shadow doubt, helped
their speedier accomplishment. The question
then comes: Is it possible, and probable, that nine
millions of men can make effective progress in
economic lines if they are deprived of political
rights, made a servile caste, and allowed only
the most meager chance for developing their
exceptional men? If history and reason give
any distinct answer to these questions, it is an
emphatic No....

The black men of America have a duty to
perform, a duty stern and delicate,—a forward
movement to oppose a part of the work of their
greatest leader [Booker T. Washington].... By
every civilized and peaceful method we must
strive for the rights which the world accords to
men, clinging unwaveringly to those great words
which the sons of the Fathers [leaders of the
American Revolution] would fain forget: "We
hold these truths to be self-evident: That all men
are created equal; they are endowed by their Creator with certain unalienable rights; that among
these are life, liberty, and the pursuit of happiness."

Source: W.E.B. DuBois, *The Souls of Black Folks.* New
York: Vintage Books, 1990, pp. 42-8.

In his 1903 essay, "The Talented Tenth," DuBois expresses his belief that blacks will achieve their goals only if they follow the "exceptional" leaders within their race.

The Negro race, like all races, is going to be saved by its exceptional men. The problem of education, then, among Negroes must first of all deal with the Talented Tenth; it is the problem of developing the Best of this race that they may guide the Mass away from the contamination and death of the Worst, in their own and other races. Now the training of men is a difficult and intricate task.... If we make money the object of man-training, we shall develop money-makers but not necessarily men; if we make technical skill the object of education, we may possess artisans but not, in nature, men. Men we shall have only as we make manhood the object of the work of the schools—intelligence, broad sympathy, knowledge of the world that was and is, and the relation of men to it—this is the curriculum of that Higher Education which must underlie true life. On this foundation we may build bread winning, skill of hand and quickness of brain, with never a fear lest the child and man mistake the means of living for the object of life....

Men of America, the problem is plain before you. Here is a race transplanted through the criminal foolishness of your fathers. Whether you like it or not the millions are here, and here they will remain. If you do not lift them up, they will pull you down. Education and work are the levers to uplift a people. Work alone will not do it unless inspired by the right ideals and guided by intelligence. Education must not simply teach work—it must teach Life. The Talented Tenth of the Negro race must be made leaders of thought and missionaries of culture among their people. No others can do this work and Negro colleges must train men for it. The Negro race, like all other races, is going to be saved by its exceptional mcn.

Consider this:
Booker T. Washington and W.E.B. DuBois both wanted blacks to succeed in life, and to work hard to attain their goals, but they had very different philosophies on how to do that. Explain each man's position in your own words, and determine which view you agree with the most.

Now, go on to read Marcus Garvey's theory on the following pages, and compare his thoughts to those of Washington and DuBois.

Source: William Dudley, ed., *African Americans: Opposing Viewpoints.* San Diego: Greenhaven Press, 1997, pp. 160-70.

Marcus Garvey

In 1917, Marcus Garvey, a native of Jamaica and founder of the black nationalist movement, established the Universal Negro Improvement Association (UNIA). His was a message of black pride, but unlike that of DuBois and other black leaders, Garvey preached separatism. Through his speeches and weekly newspaper, *The Negro World* (published in three languages), Garvey encouraged African Americans to establish their own economy separate from that of white capitalist America, and he offered blacks all over the world the vision of a new African homeland under black rule.

Garvey managed to get tremendous support from many blacks (in 1920, he boasted a membership of two million in thirty branches worldwide), but his flamboyant style and unorthodox business methods embarrassed and enraged many black intellectuals and black organizations. Garvey's movement began to lose momentum in 1925, when he was jailed for mail fraud and then deported to his home in Jamaica.

Garvey's thoughts on race relations were captured in his essay, "Aims and Objects of Movement for Solution of Negro Problem" (1923).

Summary:
The UNIA wants to improve the condition of the Negro by creating a nation in Africa where Negroes can go, without having to deal with the white race.

The Universal Negro Improvement Association is an organization among Negroes that is seeking to improve the condition of the race, with the view of establishing a nation in Africa where Negroes will be given the opportunity to develop by themselves, without creating hatred and animosity that now exist in countries of the white race through Negroes rivaling them for the highest and best positions in government, politics, society and industry. The organization believes in the rights of all men, yellow, white and black. To us, the white race has a right to the peaceful possession and occupation of countries of its own and in like manner the yellow and black races have their rights. It is only by an honest and liberal consideration of such rights can the world be blessed with the peace that is sought by Christian teachers and leaders....

The organization of the Universal Negro Improvement Association has supplied among Negroes a long-felt want. Hitherto the other Negro movements in America, with the exception of the Tuskegee effort of Booker T. Washington, sought to teach the Negro to aspire to social equality with the whites, meaning thereby the right to intermarry and fraternize in every social way. This has been the source of much trouble and still some Negro organizations continue to preach this dangerous "race destroying doctrine" added to a program of political agitation and aggression. The Universal Negro Improvement Association on the other hand believes in teaching the pride and purity of race. We believe that the white race should uphold its racial pride and perpetuate itself, and that the black race should do likewise. We believe that there is room enough in the world for the various race groups to grow and develop by themselves without seeking to destroy the Creator's plan by the constant introduction of mongrel types....

The time is opportune to regulate the relationship between both races. Let the Negro have a country of his own. Help him to return to his original home, Africa, and there give him the opportunity to climb from the lowest to the highest positions in a state of his own. If not, then the nation will have to hearken to the demand of the aggressive, "social equality" organization, known as the National Association for the Advancement of Colored People, of which W.E.B. Du Bois is leader, which declares vehemently

(continued on next page)

Summary:
They won't have to compete against whites for the best jobs.

Our organization believes in rights for all races.

In the past, others, except Washington, have advocated equality of the races, including the right to intermarry, socialize, etc. This is a source of trouble for blacks. The UNIA wants each race to remain pure. There's room enough in the world for the races to exist side-by-side without mixing.

"Let the Negro have a country of his own. Help him to return to his original home, Africa."

Vocabulary:
hitherto = until this time
perpetuate = to prolong the existence of
vehemently = forcefully, passionately

Summary:
DuBois and the NAACP want equality and the same social, political, and economic conditions for the races. That will lead to more lynchings and other troubles. The only solution is to place blacks in an environment of their own.

Vocabulary:
ascendancy = domination
viz. = that is, namely

for social and political equality, viz.—Negroes and whites in the same hotels, homes, residential districts, public and private places, a Negro as president, members of the Cabinet, Governors of States, Mayors of cities, and leaders of society in the United States.... All these, as everybody knows, are the Negroes' constitutional rights, but reason dictates that the masses of the white race will never stand by the ascendancy of an opposite minority to be the favored positions in a government, society and industry that exist by the will of the majority, hence the demand of the DuBois group of colored leaders will only lead, ultimately, to further disturbances in riots, lynching and mob rule. The only logical solution, therefore, is to supply the Negro with opportunities and environments of his own, and there[by] point him to the fullness of his ambition....

DuBois shot back at Garvey in a May 1924 editorial issue of *The Crisis.*

Summarize DuBois' response in your own words.

Marcus Garvey is, without doubt, the most dangerous enemy of the Negro race in America and in the world. He is either a lunatic or a traitor. He is sending all over this country tons of letters and pamphlets appealing to Congressmen, businessmen, philanthropists and educators to join him on a platform whose half concealed planks may be interpreted as follows:

That no person of Negro descent can ever hope to become an American citizen.

That forcible separation of the races and the banishment of Negroes to Africa is the only solution of the Negro problem.

That race war is sure to follow any attempt to realize the program of the NAACP.

We would have refused to believe that any man of Negro descent could have fathered such a propaganda if the evidence did not lie before us in black and white signed by this man....

The American Negroes have endured this

40

wretch all too long with fine restraint and every effort at cooperation and understanding. But the end has come. Every man who apologizes for or defends Marcus Garvey from this day forth writes himself down as unworthy of the countenance of decent Americans. As for Garvey himself, this open ally of the Ku Klux Klan should be locked up or sent home.

Source: William Dudley, ed., *African Americans: Opposing Viewpoints.* San Diego: Greenhaven Press, 1997, p. 200, pp.190-5.

Alain Locke and the "New Negro"

Alain Locke was the first Black Rhodes Scholar. His book, *New Negro*, a collection of poetry, essays, and art created by African Americans, led the way for the artists of the Harlem Renaissance.

...It must be increasingly recognized that the Negro has already made very substantial contributions, not only in his folk-art, music especially, which has always found appreciation, but in larger, through humbler and less acknowledged ways. For generations the Negro has been the peasant matrix of that section of America which has most undervalued him, and here he has contributed not only materially in labor and in social patience, but spiritually as well. The South has unconsciously absorbed the gift of his folk-temperament. In less than half a generation it will be easier to recognize this, but the fact remains that a leaven of humor, sentiment, imagination and tropic of nonchalance has gone into the making of the South from a humble, unacknowledged source. A second crop of the Negro's gifts promises still more largely. He now becomes a conscious contributor and lays aside the status of a beneficiary and ward for that of a collaborator and participant in American civilization.

Source: Nathan I. Huggins, ed., *Voices of the Harlem Renaissance.* NY: Oxford University Press, 1995, p. 56.

Vocabulary:
collaborator = people who work together
leaven = an element which lightens something
nonchalance = lack of concern

Harlem Renaissance - New Rhythms

by Kathryn Cryan-Hicks

The rhythms of the blues and the syncopated beats of jazz which had been carried north from the black south developed into the musical sounds of Harlem. These new sounds played out at theatres and at the many nightclubs that sprouted up in Harlem. One of the most famous clubs was the Cotton Club where "whites only" audiences were treated to the talents of black performers such as Cab Calloway and Duke Ellington. Black audiences, meanwhile, could catch their favorite acts at smaller clubs like Edmund's Cellar or Leroy's or at the popular "rent parties," where the music would continue till dawn.

Duke Ellington's career took off after his first appearance at the Cotton Club in 1927. (National African American Museum and Cultural Center)

From their main offices in New York, the NAACP and the National Urban League disseminated the message of African American pride through their monthly magazines. W.E.B. DuBois, editor of the NAACP's *The Crisis*, encouraged his readers to learn about their heritage. Charles S. Johnson, editor of the Urban League's *Opportunity*, filled his magazine with news of successful African Americans from across the nation. These magazines offered literary contests and encouraged new writers to submit their works. The careers of many of the writers we associate with the Harlem Renaissance were launched by these magazines.

The Harlem of the 1920s became a nurturing environment for young black writers. Writers like Langston Hughes, Zora Neale Hurston, Countee Cullen, Jean Toomer, and Jessie Fauset felt free to express their experiences and perspectives and to celebrate their African American heritage. Following are samples of some of the work created during this period.

"How it feels to be colored me"

Zora Neale Hurston is considered to be the most influential black woman writer before World War II. Following is an excerpt from one of her books, describing how she and a white companion reacted to the music in a jazz club.

…when I sit in the drafty basement that is The New World Cabaret [a popular nightclub in the 1920s] with a white person, my color comes. We enter chatting about any little nothing that we have in common and are seated by the jazz waiters. In the abrupt way that jazz orchestras have, this one plunges into a number. It loses no time in circumlocutions, but gets right down to business. It constricts the thorax and splits the heart with its tempo and narcotic harmonies. This orchestra grows rambunctious, rears on its hind legs and attacks the tonal veil with primitive fury, rending it, clawing it until it breaks through to the jungle beyond. I follow those heathen— follow them exultingly. I dance wildly inside myself; I yell within, I whoop; I shake my assegai above my head, I hurl it true to the mark yeeeeooww! I am in the jungle and living in the jungle way. My face is painted red and yellow and my body is painted blue. My pulse is throbbing like a war drum. I want to slaughter something—give pain, give death to what, I do not know. But the piece ends. The men of the orchestra wipe their lips and rest their fingers. I creep back slowly to the veneer we call civili- zation with the last tone and find the white friend sitting motionless in his seat-smoking calmly.

"Good music they have here," he remarks, drumming the table with his fingertips.

Music. The great blobs of purple and red emotion have not touched him. He has only heard what I felt. He is far away and I see him but dimly across the ocean and the continent that have fallen between us. He is so pale with his whiteness then and I am so colored.

Vocabulary:

assegai = a slender spear used by some South African tribes

circumlocutions = being evasive in speech, talking around something

rambunctious = boisterous, disorderly

thorax = the chest

veneer = an outward show that masks the real substance below

Source: Zora Neale Hurston, *How It Feels To Be Colored Me.* Found in *The Norton Anthology of American Literature*, Shorter Fourth Edition, New York: W.W. Norton & Company, 1995, p. 1895.

"Yet do I marvel at this curious thing:
To make a poet black, and bid him sing!"
From: "Yet Do I Marvel" by Countee Cullen

Alain Locke described Harlem this way: "Here in Manhattan is not merely the largest Negro community in the world, but the first concentration in history of so many diverse elements of Negro life.... In Harlem, Negro life is seizing upon its first chances for group expression and self-determination. It is—or promises at least to be—a race capital." Locke wrote of the renaissance, "The peasant, the student, the businessman, the professional man, artist, poet, musician, adventurer and worker, preacher and criminal, exploiter and social outcast, each group has come with its own special motives...but their greatest experience has been the finding of one another."

Langston Hughes also spoke for the blacks living in Harlem and elsewhere during the years of the Great Migration and the Depression, and he expressed their frustration and their hopes for the future. "The depression brought everybody down a peg or two. And the Negro had but few pegs to fall." *(Smithsonian web site, 1997)*

I, too

by Langston Hughes

I, too, sing America.

I am the darker brother.

They send me to eat in the kitchen

When company comes,

But I laugh,

And eat well,

And grow strong.

Tomorrow,

I'll be at the table

When company comes.

Nobody'll dare

Say to me,

"Eat in the kitchen,"

Then.

Besides,

They'll see how beautiful I am

And be ashamed —

I, too, am America.

Source: Langston Hughes, 1925, *Selected Poems*. New York: Alfred A. Knopf, Inc., 1926; renewed in 1954 by Langston Hughes. Found in *The Norton Anthology of American Literature*, Shorter Fourth Edition, New York: W.W. Norton & Company, 1995, p. 2101.

Harlem Renaissance novelist and poet Jessie Fauset was inspired by a quote from the former slave, Sojourner Truth. Truth's quote and Fauset's poem, which appeared together in *The Crisis* in January of 1920, follow.

"I can remember when I was a little, young girl, how my old mammy would sit out of doors in the evenings and look up at the stars and groan, and I would say, 'Mammy, what makes you groan so?'" And she would say, 'I am groaning to think of my poor children; they do not know where I be and I don't know where they be. I look up at the stars and they look up at the stars!'"

— Sojourner Truth

Oriflamme

by Jessie Fauset

I think I see her sitting bowed and black,
Stricken and seared with slavery's mortal scars,
Reft of her children, lonely, anguished, yet
Still looking at the stars.

Symbolic mother, we thy myriad sons,
Pounding our stubborn hearts on Freedom's bars,
Clutching our birthright, fight with faces set,
Still visioning the stars!

Source: Jessie Fauset, "Oriflamme," *The Crisis*, New York: January 1920.

Vocabulary:

Oriflamme = "flame of gold," (French) refers to an ancient banner of the kings of France, which was said to have the power to blind infidels who looked at it, or to envelope them in a mist.

reft = deprived of

45

Saturday's Child

by Countee Cullen

Vocabulary:
opulent = wealthy

Some are teethed on a silver spoon,
With the stars strung for a rattle;
I cut my teeth as the black raccoon—
For implements of battle.

Some are swaddled in silk and down,
And heralded by a star;
They swathed my limbs in a sackcloth gown
On a night that was black as tar.

For some, godfather and goddame
The opulent fairies be;
Dame Poverty gave me my name,
And Pain godfathered me.

For I was born on Saturday—
"Bad time for planting a seed,"
Was all my father had to say,
And, "One mouth more to feed."

Death cut the strings that gave me life,
And handed me to Sorrow,
The only kind of middle wife
My folks could beg or borrow.

The Lynching
by Claude McKay

His spirit in smoke ascended to high heaven.
His father, by the cruelest way of pain,
Had bidden him to his bosom once again;
The awful sin remained still unforgiven.
All night a bright and solitary star
(Perchance the one that ever guided him,
Yet gave him up at last to Fate's wild whim)
Hung pitifully o'er the swinging char.
Day dawned, and soon the mixed crowds came
    to view
The ghastly body swaying in the sun:
The women thronged to look, but never a one
Showed sorrow in her eyes of steely blue;
And little lads, lynchers that were to be,
Danced around the dreadful thing in fiendish glee.

Source: "The Lynching" by Claude McKay, *Selected Poems* by Claude McKay. Copyright 1953, Twayne Publishers.

After every lynching, the NAACP flew this flag outside its NYC office. (Library of Congress)

Dream Deferred

by Kathryn Cryan-Hicks

The spirit of the Harlem of the twenties provided a colorful backdrop for this creative explosion of black art we know as the Harlem Renaissance. Yet in the thirties, that backdrop fell heavily with the Great Depression.

The promise that glowed during the Harlem Renaissance was obscured by a harsher light of reality. Publishing and performing opportunities decreased as money became scarce everywhere. Writers became more preoccupied with the social and economic realities and their themes displayed little of the hope and optimisim of earlier works.

Harlem

by Langston Hughes

What happens to a dream deferred?

Does it dry up
like a raisin in the sun?
Or fester like a sore—
And then run?
Does it stink like rotten meat?
Or crust and sugar over
like a syrupy sweet?
Maybe it just sags
like a heavy load.

Or does it explode?

Epilogue
by Mitch Yamasaki, Ph.D.

The Great Migration had a profound impact on the history of the United States in the twentieth century. First, it transformed race relations from a "southern problem" to a national issue. The struggles of the post-World War II Civil Rights Movement were fought on the streets of Chicago, Boston, and New York, as well as Birmingham, Little Rock, and Jackson. Second, it accelerated the demographic shift of poverty from rural to urban America. Poverty still exists in rural regions. But the largest concentrations of poverty and crime are now found in the nation's inner cities. This is where the poorest and most vulnerable blacks live.

Finally, African American culture prior to the Great Migration was dispersed and regional. The migration brought about a cultural fusion within the black community, which produced some of America's finest literature and music.

"During the Harlem Renaissance, intellectual dialogue, literary and artistic creation, blues and jazz, dance and musical theater came together and flowered as never before. There were active offices of the National Association for the Advancement of Colored People, the Urban League, and the Universal Negro Improvement Association. There were all black musicals, dance clubs, jazz clubs, and nightclubs that catered to whites. The leaders and stars are still known today....

"Ultimately, the Depression, unemployment, poverty, gang violence, and most of all segregation—not legal segregation but the continuing inequality between whites and blacks—changed Harlem in the 1930s, and it became a sad and dangerous place. Despite so many brilliant accomplishments, there was no fundamental change in the comparative position of the two races."

Source of last two paragraphs: Smithsonian Institution Homepage, 1997.

Research Activities/Things to Do

- Describe in your own words the "push" and "pull" that led to the Great Migration of African Americans from the rural South to the urban North.

- Beyond the availability of jobs in the North, what were some of the new experiences and opportunities for southern blacks when they migrated North?

- "Jim Crow" laws mandated that blacks have separate facilities for travel, lodging, eating and drinking, schooling, worship, housing, and other aspects of social and economic life. What effect did the "Jim Crow" laws have on blacks who left the South expecting racial equality?

- The letters found in the *Chicago Defender* show the desperate desire of blacks to move North—for jobs and other opportunities. Assume the situation is reversed, today. You are a young black person, living in a crowded city, with no job opportunity, and a bleak outlook for getting out of your present situation. Write a "Letter to the Editor" of a rural southwestern newspaper, convincing her/him that you would be a great person to hire in a local business.

- Do you think that the harsh treatment of blacks in the South or the opportunity for economic advancement in the North was the stronger motivating force for the Great Migration? Give concrete examples that back up your point-of-view.

- Why did the blacks of the rural South look at the urban centers of the North as "The Promised Land?"

- Although blacks found jobs in factories, on assembly lines, and in domestic service, they rarely rose to management positions. Why?

- In the years following the end of the Civil War, life for former slaves improved little in the South. Unable to work for decent wages, denied equality in education, and abused by growing racial prejudice and violence, blacks moved North and to the Midwest by the tens of thousands. Make a graph from the figures given in the report by W.E.B. DuBois (pages 14 to 15) of the numbers leaving from various departure points.

- Summarize the reasons given for leaving the South.

- Blacks arriving in cities like New York and Chicago settled in African American neighborhoods, where housing was less expensive, and the "community" felt more comfortable. Compare this grouping to that of the European immigrants who settled in our nation prior to and following the black migration north.

- Did the opportunities in the North pan out to be all that the blacks had hoped and expected they would be? Explain your answer with citations from primary sources.

- As more blacks moved North, racial violence and prejudice increased. Blacks banded together to take a firm political and social stance. At other times in recent history, blacks have rioted and/or protested their lack of equal opportunities. Find the common threads behind these demonstrations throughout the 20th century.

- How did Marcus Garvey's philosophy differ from that of other black leaders, such as Booker T. Washington or W.E.B. DuBois?

- A spirit of black pride flourished in Harlem after the migration north. Despite the social and political turmoil of the period, black artists, musicians, and poets made significant contributions to American culture that are still recognized today. Choose a particular artist to study, and report on his or her artistic contributions.

BALLAD OF BOOKER T.   *1st draft*
                                       May 30, 1941

Old Booker T.

Was a practical man.

He said, Till the soil,

Le rn from the land.

Let down your buckets

Where you are;

In your own backyard

There ~~could~~

~~might~~ be a star.

Train you ~~be~~ *head*

Your ~~head~~ *heart*, ~~and~~ your hand.

To help yourself

And your fellowman

Thus Booker T.

Built a school.

~~With~~ Book-learning there

And the workman's tool.

He started out

In a simple way:--

For ~~Y~~Yesterday

Was not today.

Sometimes he had ~~to~~

~~Co~~promise in his talk;--

For a man must crawl

Before he can walk

And in Alabama in '85

A joker was lucky
          be
To ~~stay~~ alive.

But ~~ald~~ Booker T.

Was nobody's fool:

You may carve a dream

From an humble tool--

And the tallest tower

Can tumble down

If ~~in~~ *not* rooted

In solid ground.

He said, Train your ~~heart~~, *head*)

*For the smart alone
Is ~~not~~ rarely meet---
~~When~~/you haven't got
/Something to eat.*

*Train your he
Your ~~head~~ heart, and your hand.--
For Booker T.
Was a practical man.*

[LC70549]

Source: Library of Congress

• Evaluate this poem by Langston Hughes using the worksheet on page 53.

Analyzing Poems Worksheet

1. **Time period from which the poem comes:**

2. **Date(s) or other markings on poem:**
    ❏ No Date   ❏ Copyright   ❏ Other_____

3. **What do you know about the poet?**

4. **For what audience was the piece written?**

5. **Key Information** (In your opinion, what is the message of the poem?)

6. **Do you think the poem was spontaneously written? Why or why not?**

7. **Choose a quote from the piece that helped you to know why it was written:**

8. **Write down two clues which you got from the words that tell you something about life in the U. S. at the time it was written:**

9. **What is the mood of the poem?**

10. **Does the wording have any symbolic meaning?**

11. **If the poem is a draft, analyze and comment on the changes made by the poet.**

Above: The 1930s were a time when African-Americans became more active—and accepted—in the organized labor movements and were sufficiently confident to go on strike over pay and conditions. (Library of Congress) ***Below:*** *Women in the South had little enthusiasm or hope for the menial tasks they performed.* (National Archives)

• Evaluate these photos using the worksheet on page 55.

Analyzing Photos Worksheet

Some or all of the following will help you to analyze an historic photo, or other type of graphic. Use the worksheet to jot down notes about each piece being evaluated.

1. **What is the subject matter? Compare the two photos to each other.**

2. **What details provide clues?**

    ❏ scene   ❏ buildings   ❏ people

    ❏ clothing   ❏ artifacts   ❏ time of day

    ❏ style of graphic ❏ written message   ❏ season

    ❏ B&W/color

3. **Can you determine the locations?   The intended audiences?**

4. **What is the date? If there is no date, can you guess the period?**

5. **What is the purpose of the photos?**

    ❏ private use   ❏ recording an event ❏ propaganda

    ❏ art   ❏ advertising   ❏ Other_____

6. **Can you tell anything about the point of view of the graphics?**

7. **What details make these pieces effective or ineffective?**

8. **What can you learn about the people who lived at this time from the photos?**

9. **Which setting has more hope? Why? What do the peoples' facial expressions tell you about their lives? Explain your answer.**

Suggested Further Reading

The books listed below are suggested readings in American literature, which tie in with the *Researching American History Series*. The selections were made based on feedback from teachers and librarians currently using them in interdisciplinary classes for students in grades 5 to 12. Of course there are many other historical novels that would be appropriate to tie in with the titles in this series.

Northern Migration and the Harlem Renaissance

Fauset, Jessie Redmon, *There is confusion; Plum Bun; The China Tree; Comedy, American Style*

Fisher, Rudolph, *The Walls of Jericho; The Conjure Man Dies: A Mystery Tale of Dark Harlem,*

Hughes, Langston: *Not Without Laughter*

Hurston, Zora Neale: *Jonah's Gourd Wine; Their Eyes Were Watching God*

Larsen, Nella: *Quicksand; Passing*

McKay, Claude: *Home to Harlem; Banjo; Gingertown; Banana Bottom*

Schuyler, George: *Black No More; Slaves Today*

Thurman, Wallace: *The Blacker the Berry - a Novel of Negro Life; Infants of the Spring; Interne, with Abraham l. Furman*

Toomer, Jean: *Cane*

Van Vechten, Carl: *Nigger Heaven*

Walrond, Eric: *Tropic Death*

White, Walter: *The Fire in the Flint; Flight*

Wright, Richard: *Native Son*

For information on these and other titles from Discovery Enterprises, Ltd., call or write to: Discovery Enterprises, Ltd., 31 Laurelwood Drive, Carlisle, MA 01741 Phone: 978-287-5401 Fax: 978-287-5402